101 THING
NOT TO S
DURING SEX

CHRISTMAS 1996.

To 'LINZ' WITH 'LURVE'

. THERE APPEARS TO BE ONE
"THING" MISSING.....

I GUESS IT MUST BE
IN "102 THINGS NOT TO
SAY DURING SEX" !!! ...

HAVE A GIGGLE & MAKE
NOTES .... Andy x.

101 THINGS NOT TO SAY DURING SEX

Patti Putnicki

Illustrations by Dusty Rumsey

PENGUIN BOOKS

PENGUIN BOOKS

Published by the Penguin Group
Penguin Books Ltd, 27 Wrights Lane, London W8 5TZ, England
Penguin Books USA Inc., 375 Hudson Street, New York, New York 10014, USA
Penguin Books Australia Ltd, Ringwood, Victoria, Australia
Penguin Books Canada Ltd, 10 Alcorn Avenue, Toronto, Ontario, Canada M4V 3B2
Penguin Books (NZ) Ltd, 182–190 Wairau Road, Auckland 10, New Zealand

Penguin Books Ltd, Registered Offices: Harmondsworth, Middlesex, England

First published in the USA by Warner Books 1993
First published in Great Britain by Penguin Books 1993
9 10

Printed in England by Clays Ltd, St Ives plc

Patti and Dusty wish to thank the following individuals for their support and encouragement:

Joseph S. Ajlouny, our agent; Mauro DiPreta, our editor;
Brian Healy, our production coordinator;
Jerry Jenkins and Jeff Soper, our mentors;
and to Gwen, Elena, Jan, Bryan, Cheryl, Gary, Robert and Donna, who taught us "not to say" so much.
We also wish to thank all the folks who have never said any of the things we've described herein. You are a credit to your race even if you are too polite to be any fun at all.

101 THINGS
NOT TO SAY
DURING SEX

3

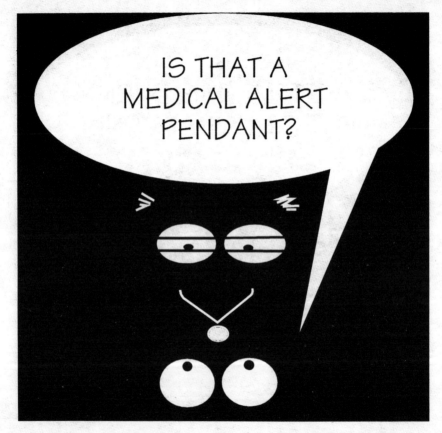

8

19

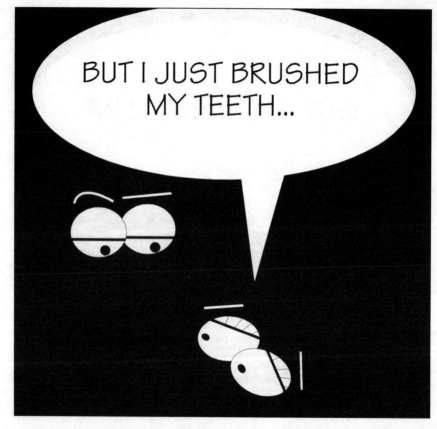

36

43

46

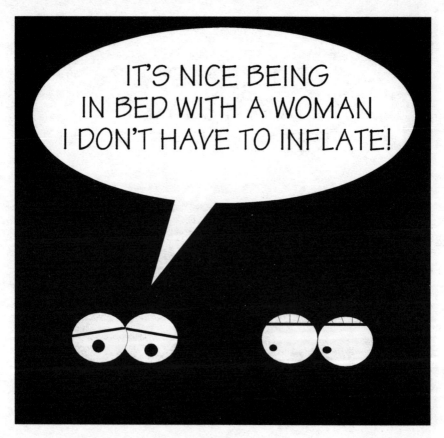

48

49

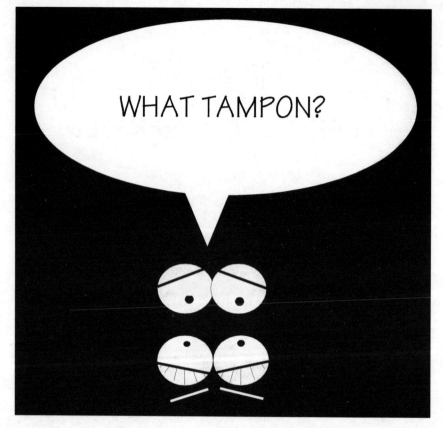

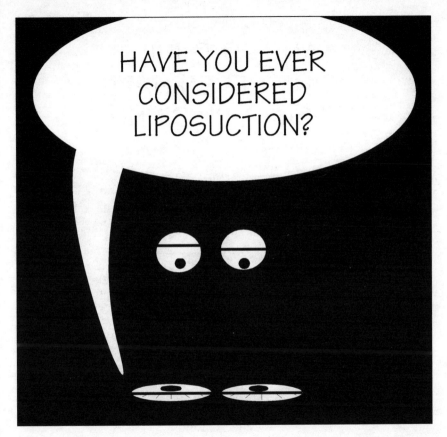

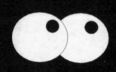

77

79

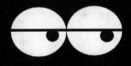

85

93

95

97